FIGURES IN STONE

ARCHITECTURAL SCULPTURE IN NEW YORK CITY

ROBERT ARTHUR KING

FOREWORD BY BARRY LEWIS

This book is dedicated with thanks and appreciation to two people who are very important to me for very different reasons:

Inge M. Zenner, whose friendship I am enjoying after a 43-year delay, and her husband, Claus L. Arentoft.

Joseph Vescio, for his dedication to and investment in our working relationship.

In addition, I thank my wife, Elinor M. King, for tolerating my obsession with collecting
photographs of building details in as many cities as possible.

Previous pages: see page 104.

Copyright © 2017, 2009, 2008 by Robert Arthur King
Copyright © 2009, 2008 by W. W. Norton & Company, Inc.
Maps copyright © 2009, 2008 by W. W. Norton & Company, Inc.

Previously published in ANIMALS IN STONE (2009) and FACES IN STONE (2008)

For information about permission to reproduce selections from this book, write to
Permissions, W. W. Norton & Company, Inc., 500 Fifth Avenue, New York, NY 10110

For information about special discounts for bulk purchases, please contact W. W. Norton
Special Sales at specialsales@wwnorton.com or 800-233-4830

Manufacturing by KHL
Book design by Eleen Chung
Production manager: Leeann Graham

Library of Congress Cataloging-in-Publication Data

Names: King, Robert Arthur, 1945- author. | Container of: King, Robert Arthur, 1945- Animals in stone. | Container of: King, Robert Arthur, 1945- Faces in stone.
Title: Figures in stone : architectural sculpture in New York City / Robert Arthur King ; foreword by Barry Lewis.
Description: First edition. | New York : W.W. Norton & Company, 2017. |
"Previously published as ANIMALS IN STONE (2009) and FACES IN STONE (2008)."
Identifiers: LCCN 2016055350 | ISBN 9780393712438 (pbk.)
Subjects: LCSH: Decoration and ornament, Architectural--New York
(State)--New York. | Sculpture--New York (State)--New York. | New York (N.Y.)--Buildings, structures, etc.
Classification: LCC NA3511.N48 K565 2017 | DDC 729.09747--dc23 LC record available at https://lccn.loc.gov/2016055350
ISBN: 978-0-393-71243-8 (pbk.)

W. W. Norton & Company, Inc., 500 Fifth Avenue, New York, N.Y. 10110
www.wwnorton.com

W. W. Norton & Company Ltd., 15 Carlisle Street, London W1D 3BS

1 2 3 4 5 6 7 8 9 0

PREFACE

❧

"The camera is no more an instrument of preservation, the image is."   —Berenice Abbott

"Every building must have . . . its own soul."   —Louis Kahn

After the publication of *Faces in Stone* and *Animals in Stone*, I expanded my search for building details to cities in America (Chicago, Philadelphia, Seattle, etc.) and Europe (Madrid, Copenhagen, Stockholm, etc.). I discovered that New York City is not alone in destroying buildings, with no regard for the preservation of historic details. Although European cities are more committed to preservation than America, many pieces of immense interest are still vulnerable. Modern architecture unfortunately lacks the visual sophistication provided by informative and artistic details available on older buildings. The sterility of new buildings displays no education about their use or function.

Regrettably, the anonymous craftsmen who executed these wonderfully vital and useful details are gone. Their work, which is their legacy, should not be forgotten. We can continue to appreciate their work and be grateful for each piece that can and should be salvaged even if only through photographs.

FOREWORD

by Barry Lewis

Robert Arthur King's photos are a record of a disappearing city. If only the camera existed before the modern era so we could have recorded the details of ancient Babylon, Rome, or medieval Paris. At least in other parts of the world, buildings from the past are more likely to be respected and taken care of. Here, in the States, we prefer to demolish what's there and build something new. No city exemplifies the American need to swap out the old for the new better than New York itself. Since most of Mr. King's photographs are of non-landmark-designated buildings here in a city almost under siege from gentrification, these details and the structures they ornament are likely to be gone before this century is half over.

The "Figures in Stone" Mr. King has captured are on buildings built in the late 19th or early 20th century. It was a special time in architectural history, at least here in the West. The architectural movement of the time was called "Eclecticism," an era that lasted a little over 100 years from the early 19th century to the mid 20th. Acting as rebels and provocateurs, the Eclectics went up against the 400-year-old Renaissance formulas of design that brought a universal language of architecture (and the other arts as well) to the muddled and bloodied field of medieval Europe. These formulas said that even if war and strife remain, at least in architecture—and the arts—we could find harmony, balance, and reason. That was lovely, except after four centuries of hewing to that formula, the "harmony & balance" sought by the Establishment had become a strait-jacket of sorts, a crustaceous shell that sealed all "architecture" in the same rigid box.

The Eclectics were the 'punks' of their day vis-à-vis the Beaux-Arts Establishment of that time going up against the stalwarts of the Academy. But they weren't being outrageous just for the kick of it. They understood that with the coming Industrial Revolution and the triumph of the middle class as the reigning power of the 19th century, new types of buildings were needed—corporate headquarters, merchant exchanges, public art galleries, museums and libraries, public hospitals, rail-road stations, and, not least, suburban houses for the wealthy business classes. These buildings needed to be flexible—easy to expand or change as uses and business practices, families and their retinue, changed from generation to generation. The rising bourgeoisie was replacing the old status quo of aristocrats and monarchs that had held fast for generations, and architecture had to serve the new ruling class's very different needs.

The Eclectics also understood that in this increasingly mechanized society, where business buildings, houses, and their furnishings were products of a machine, the "sameness" of everything, the mass-production of everything, threatened to obliterate our individualism....our uniqueness.

The Eclectics believed that there was not one accepted universal style as the Renaissance had dictated; to the contrary, "style" was relative depending on the purpose of the building, where it sat, and who would be using it. The Eclectics brought in the notion that every building—like every person—was unique and that its architectural style and decoration should reflect that uniqueness.

Different architectural styles were used—Greek Revival, neo-Gothic, Italianate, etc.—for different situations, whether city or country, home or business, top-of-the-hill or down-in-the–valley. Towers and turrets were happily grouped into silhouettes giving the building a distinctive skyline, allowing the building a unique plan tailored to its use and also making it more amenable to future possible expansion. Sculptural figures were added to give both the building in total and each corner a uniqueness that defined its very special place in the universe.

Sculptural elements could be just about anything. Human "head-shots," animals of every kind, abstract arabesques, "grotesques" that laughed at us or the human condition—all were acceptable to make the building special. Sometimes the sculptural ornament played on themes of the building's location, perhaps its builders or hopefully its future tenants, or simply conveyed "unique-i-tude." Everything the architects did was to give each building "specialness."

Now we live in a very different world. The Modern Movement (some think of it as Mid-Century Modern) triumphed in the middle of the 20th century and brought us back to the Renaissance ideal of a *universal language of architecture*. That "language" is supposedly based on "minimalism" and "function." Though Modern buildings can be exhilarating (see the work of masters like Louis Kahn, the finessed details of a Mies van der Rohe, the explosive vigor of Luis Barragan or an Oscar Niemeyer), too often Modern means banal, boring, and blank (don't even ask about dysfunctional). The buildings going up in New York today, whether along Sixth Avenue in the former Flower District, the West Side Yards, or in the vicinity of the new World Trade Center, could be *anywhere*, from Dubai to Shanghai to London's Canary Wharf.

We have gone from the "specific" of the Eclectics to the "universalism" of the Modern, but the triumph of those universalisms have led us to a crushing sameness, a boring sense of "nowhere-ness"—or perhaps a sense of "everywhere-ness"—where one high-rise skyline looks much like another,

The Eclectics created a sense of place that visually defined a city. Boston's Eclecticism does not look like Philadelphia's, or San Francisco's, or New York's. Even the small towns of America created an Eclectic architecture that visually defined their special place. When we lose these buildings—and their details so intriguingly created by their builders, and now captured in "portraits" by Mr. King—we lose that special sense of place they visually conveyed. And we have lost it forever.

That's why we need this book. To record what we have taken away from ourselves. Each time we demolish one of these buildings, and destroy its joyful congregation of sculpted souls, we chip away a little bit more at the place we call New York.

I'm not a Luddite. I'm a New Yorker born and raised. I understand that things change, none more so than the city I call home. But are we aware of what we are losing every time one of Mr. King's subjects is smashed to powder? Whether we are natives of this city, long-time adoptees, or simply people who love this place but can't figure out why, we are losing a little bit of ourselves as these unique, Eclectic details disappear.

When it's all gone and we only have photographic essays like Mr. King's of "what-was" we can wonder at the craziness of these Eclectic builders, that they were so lavish in their ornamental details, marvel at their sometimes wacky, sometimes sober sculptural portraits. Those coming in the future, who will know a city of literally faceless facades, might be puzzled by the extravagance of those who came before them. But in a sense it was no different than the current generation's obsession with tattoos and piercings: in an undifferentiated sea of sameness, these sculptural details gave us a unique sense of place and existence.

At least we will have photographic records like Robert Arthur King's to know what we have lost.

FACES IN STONE

ARCHITECTURAL SCULPTURE IN NEW YORK CITY

W. W. NORTON
NEW YORK · LONDON

PREFACE

❧

"The creation of art is not the fulfillment of a need but the creation of a need." —Louis I. Kahn

This book started years ago as a photography class assignment that just grew and grew. The assignment was to photograph women. I don't like photographing people, so my solution was to take the photos of women's faces on buildings. The instructor was surprised by my end run around his request, but pleased with the results.

The assignment focused my attention on building details all over New York City, and I spent hours over the next few years recording faces, finding them more and more intriguing. Who carved or sculpted these details? Why? Did the faces represent specific people?

Sometimes research provided answers. For example, the faces on the Woolworth Building, 229-237 Broadway, include the owner, the architect, and the builder. Their visages will remind observers of their existence as long as the building stands! The building at 45 Monroe Street displays the face of the developer, a signature for his work. Sometimes the sculptures depict the children or family members of the property owner—for example, at 120 Riverside Drive, Manhattan, and 156 Prospect Park West, Brooklyn. Other sites recognize particular types rather than individuals: the carvings on the Montauk Club, 25 Eighth Avenue, Brooklyn, are Native Americans, specifically members of the Montauk tribe from the tip of Long Island.

Most of the buildings with sculpted decorative details were built during the years between the Civil War and World War I, a period that included the storied Gilded Age, when an influx of European emigrants, among them many skilled craftsmen, provided the wherewithal to embellish the dwellings and businesses of newly affluent citizens. The ornate and sometimes ostentatious details were designed for entrances, around doorways, on cornices, and in lobbies. Classic Greek and Roman images were particularly popular. The wonderful ornamentation, whether beautiful women's faces or frightening grotesques, or natural elements such as acanthus leaves, vines, and flowers, was intended to impress visitors and residents, and still does.

Many of the buildings so decorated have been torn down, but many remain for the observant to enjoy. Their condition ranges from the well maintained to the derelict. Only serious attention by concerned citizens will save the most vulnerable ones. If taste, style, and cost have eliminated such architectural detail from modern architecture as indicated by the current prevalent blank-faced, repetitive buildings, there is all the more reason to salvage and preserve for posterity the legacy left to us by the profoundly talented but largely anonymous craftsmen whose work we admire so much.

THE FACES THAT YOU MEET

by Allison Silver, Politics Producer, Charlie Rose

Though the prototype of the modern city, New York is decidedly Old World. For example, it is ideal for pedestrian traffic. It is also a metropolis of soft watercolors, not the hard Day-glo colors of other New World cities like Los Angeles or Las Vegas or Miami. Rather, New York's Beaux-Arts behemoths and stately brownstones are designed in muted colors and sepia tones.

These buildings are old-fashioned, steadfast structures, built on rock-solid foundations. They hearken back to the Gilded Age, the bustling Gotham of ruthless plutocrats proclaiming their legacy, substantial burghers asserting their prosperity, and working-class strivers struggling for a toehold—a New York not unlike that of today.

Yet these stolid buildings, seemingly so sturdy and impassive, are often adorned with fantastical beings, carved out of stone or molded in terra cotta that call out to modern passersby, telling of the New York of dreams, a city of wonder and enchantment.

They are storied creatures from another time: fauns and nymphs, satyrs and naiads, conquistadors and Native Americans, gods and goddesses. They testify to a magical city where anything is possible—where a shoeshine boy can become a titan of industry, a nimble storyteller an influential novelist, a shy small-town girl the sophisticated toast of the town. They speak to the myths that drew people to the city, myths that create a great city.

A real city, we know, is always about change: people are transformed in the cauldron of the melting pot. Yet these ornamental faces who watch over the change are eternal and immutable, from long-told tales. In a city where little stays the same, they do. They are hidden in plain sight, on capitals and plaques, capstones and cornices. They seem to offer age-old wisdom as they survey the fast urban pace, yet remain apart from it.

The faces shown here are New World variations on gargoyles. They are not gargoyles in the traditional meaning of that word. True, many have their mouths open, wildly laughing or crying (in a sort of precursor to painter Edvard Munch's "Scream" series), but these are not fanciful downspouts for rainwater. They are not there to ward off evil. Most are grotesques or humoresques, with misshapen or idiosyncratic, exotic or whimsical faces. Still others are beautiful women with classic features and serene (if stony) brows. Many of the faces, even those so clearly depicting late nineteenth- or early twentieth-century tycoons, are framed by swirls of cascading curls. Some are crowned with laurel wreaths. Venerable gentlemen have remarkable beards or assertive mustaches. Sweet-faced children are frozen, unmoving in a most unchildlike manner. Specific artists are memorialized, painters such as Rembrandt and Whistler. And, on Riverside Drive, all the arts of the city are honored—a chef as well as a painter, an architect, a carpenter.

Some figures have a syncopated, Jazz Age feel—like a remarkable visage on Broome Street, peaking out from a machine-age motif. Others are as neoclassical as profiles on a Roman coin. Still others are pre-Raphaelite, dreamy and ethereal. They surprise and delight—Hercules in his lion's skin is no less expected than Teddy Roosevelt.

The faces can appear randomly or surreptitiously. You are walking along when, suddenly, you spot a face laughing down or grimacing out at you. Then, the most mundane of buildings becomes extraordinary—dashing or natty or elegant.

In a city, they say, you can be lonely, but never alone. You are always one among many. But look at this another way. One of the joys of New York is that, in so many neighborhoods, on so many different streets, even when no other people are around, you are forever a face in the crowd.

Note: Unless otherwise specified, addresses are in Manhattan.

For maps showing the location of the faces and an index to the addresses, see pages 142-144.

106 Prospect Park West, Brooklyn

Subway: Bus: B69

Map #2

502 12 Street, Brooklyn

Subway: **F**   Bus: B69, B75

Map #6

25 Eighth Avenue, Brooklyn

Subway: ② ③ Bus: B41, B67

Map #13

Map #60

11

480 Park Avenue

Map #49

28 Prospect Park West, Brooklyn

Map #1

521 12 Street, Brooklyn

Subway: **F** Bus: B69

Map #8

429 3 Street, Brooklyn

Subway: F M R Bus: B63

Map #14

485 13 Street, Brooklyn

Map #7

584 11 Street, Brooklyn

Subway: **F**   Bus: B69

Map #9

121 Prospect Park West, Brooklyn

Subway: **F**   Bus: B69

Map #3

257 West 116 Street

Map #80

816 Eighth Avenue, Brooklyn

Subway: F Bus: B69

Map #10

164 Prospect Park West, Brooklyn

Map #5

371 East 138 Street, Bronx

Subway: **6** Bus: BX15, BX33

Map #1

218 St. Ann's Avenue, Bronx

Map #2

1 Park Avenue

Subway: **6** Bus: M1

Map #39

930 Lexington Avenue

Subway: **6** Bus: M98, M101, M102, M103

Map #50

198 Eighth Avenue, Brooklyn

Subway: Bus: B69

Map #11

202 Eighth Avenue, Brooklyn

Subway: 2 3 F   Bus: B69

Map #12

165 Orchard Street

Subway: F V J M Z

Bus: M15

Map #30

375 Broome Street

Subway: J M Z Bus: M103

Map #23

7 Elizabeth Street

Subway: Bus: M103

Map #20

5 Washington Place

Subway: Bus: M9

Map #34

25 Henry Street

Subway: (F) Bus: M15, M22

Map #3

13 Division Street

Subway: F J M Z   Bus: M15

Map #17

26 Jefferson Street

Subway: Bus: M22

Map #6

Map #87

35

9 Henry Street

Subway: **F** **J** **M** **Z**

Bus: M15

Map #2

38 Jefferson Street

Map #11

27 Rutgers Street

Subway: **F**   Bus: M22

Map #13

35 Henry Street

Subway: **F** Bus: M15, M22

Map #3

58 East 1 Street

Map #31

Map #73

45 Monroe Street

Subway:  Bus: M15, M22

Map #1

52 Mott Street

Subway: J M Z Bus: M103

Map #19

56 Henry Street

Map #4

15 Eldridge Street

Map #16

122 Forsyth Street

Subway: J M Z Bus: M15

Map #28

73 Eldridge Street

Map #26

75 Central Park West

Subway: ① Ⓑ Ⓒ Bus: M10, M72

Map #59

76 West 85 Street

Map #66

50

78 West 85 Street

Subway: Ⓑ Ⓒ Bus: M7, M11

Map #66

2154 Frederick Douglass Boulevard

Map #81

96 East Broadway

Map #15

104 Forsyth Street

Map #27

156 Prospect Park West, Brooklyn

Map #4

55

111 Henry Street

Subway:  F   Bus: M15, M22

Map #5

111 Manhattan Avenue

Subway: Ⓐ Ⓑ Ⓒ Ⓓ

Bus: M7, M10, M11

Map #72

310 St. Nicholas Avenue

Subway: Bus: M3

Map #86

Map #70

121 Henry Street

Subway: F Bus: M15, M22

Map #5

129 West 86 Street

Subway: **1** **B** **C**

Bus: M7, M11, M86

Map #67

123 West 86 Street

Map #67

225 West 106 Street

Subway: Bus: M7, M11

Map #76

130-132 Eldridge Street

Subway:  Bus: M9

Map #29

157 East 86 Street

Subway:

Bus: M86, M101, M102, M103

Map #56

162 Henry Street

Subway: **F** Bus: M15, M22

Map #5

376 Lafayette Street

Subway: Bus: M1

Map #33

69

214–218 Mulberry Street

Subway: **6** Bus: M1

Map #25

Map #5

173–185 Fifth Avenue

Subway: R W 6 Bus: M1, M2, M3

Map #36

181 Mott Street

Subway: J M Z 6
Bus: M103

Map #22

73

211 Madison Street

Subway: Ⓕ Bus: M22

Map #12

197–199 Madison Street

Subway: **6** Bus: M1, M2, M3

Map #14

201 West 79 Street

Subway:  **1** Bus: M5, M79

Map #63

225 West 86 Street

Subway: ① Bus: M7, M11, M86

Map #68

191 Henry Street

Subway: **F**   Bus: M22

Map #9

205 West 77 Street

Subway: 1 Bus: M7, M11

Map #61

221 Madison Street

Subway:  Bus: M22

Map #10

223 Madison Street

Map #10

239 Central Park West

Subway: B C Bus: M10

Map #64

241 Henry Street

Subway: **F**   Bus: M22

Map #8

250 West 77 Street

Map #62

251 East Broadway

Map #7

255 West 108 Street

Subway: ① Bus: M4, M60, M104

Map #78

256 West 145 Street

Subway: ③ Ⓐ Ⓑ Ⓒ Ⓓ
Bus: M10, M12, BX19

Map #95

108 Edgecombe Avenue

Subway: Bus: M3

Map #98

102 Edgecombe Avenue

Subway: Ⓐ Ⓑ Ⓒ Ⓓ Bus: M3

Map #98

260 Convent Avenue

Subway: ① Ⓐ Ⓑ Ⓒ Ⓓ

Bus: M18, M100, M101

Map #90

284 Fifth Avenue

Subway: 6 R W
Bus: M2, M3, M5

Map #38

4 East 39 Street

Subway:  4 5 6 7

Bus: M1, M2, M3, M4, M5

Map #41

315 Park Avenue South

Subway: **6** Bus: M1

Map #37

351 East 52 Street

Subway: 6 E V Bus: M15

Map #44

Map #84

362 Broome Street

Subway: J M Z Bus: M103

Map #21

368 Convent Avenue

Subway: (A) (B) (C) (D)

Bus: M18, M100, M101, BX19

Map #92

370 Park Avenue

Subway: 6 E V
Bus: M1, M2, M3

Map #43

890 Fifth Avenue

Map #53

Map #88

473 West 145 Street

Subway: Ⓐ Ⓑ Ⓒ Ⓓ

Bus: M18, M100, M101, BX19

Map #91

390-394 Broome Street

Subway: 6 J M Z Bus: M103

Map #24

411-413 Fifth Avenue

Subway: 6 B D F V N R W Q

Bus: M2, M3

Map #40

418 Convent Avenue

Subway: Ⓐ Ⓑ Ⓒ Ⓓ
Bus: M18, M100, M101

Map #93

5 Elizabeth Street

Subway: Bus: M103

Map #20

450–454 Avenue of the Americas

Subway: Ⓐ Ⓑ Ⓒ Ⓓ Ⓔ Ⓕ Ⓥ ① Bus: M5, M6

Map #35

452 Fifth Avenue

Subway: B D F V 7
Bus: M2, M3

Map #42

463 Seventh Avenue

Subway: ① ② ③ Bus: M10, M20

Map #45

7-9 Chatham Square

Subway: Ⓙ Ⓜ Ⓩ Bus: M9

Map #18

475 West 145 Street

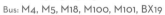

Subway:  Ⓐ Ⓑ Ⓒ Ⓓ

Bus: M4, M5, M18, M100, M101, BX19

Map #91

540 Manhattan Avenue

Subway: Ⓐ Ⓑ Ⓒ Ⓓ   Bus: M3, M18

Map #85

495 West End Avenue

Subway: **1** Bus: M5

Map #69

521 West 145 Street

Subway: **1**

Bus: M4, M5, M100, M101, BX19

Map #94

523 West 134 Street

Subway: **1**
Bus: M4, M5, M100, M101, BX19

Map #88

527 Cathedral Parkway

Subway: **1** Bus: M4, M11

Map #79

Map #52

557 Eighth Avenue

Subway: Bus: M20

Map #46

285 Central Park West

Map #65

644 Broadway

Subway: 6 B D F V
Bus: M1, M6

Map #32

778 Park Avenue

Subway: Bus: M1, M2, M3, M4

Map #55

2495-2499 Adam Clayton Powell Boulevard

Subway:  Bus: M2, BX19

Map #96

817 West End Avenue

Subway: ① ② ③ Bus: M5, M104

Map #71

801 West End Avenue

Map #71

909–917 Columbus Avenue

Subway: **1** **B** **C** Bus: M7, M11, M16

Map #74

Map #97

925 West End Avenue

Subway: Bus: M5, M104

Map #77

1947 Adam Clayton Powell Boulevard

Map #82

912 Amsterdam Avenue

Map #75

Map #51

1971 Adam Clayton Powell Boulevard

Subway:  Bus: M2

Map #83

1377 Lexington Avenue

Subway: 4 5 6

Bus: M98, M101, M102, M103

Map #58

1534 Third Avenue

Subway: 4 5 6

Bus: M98, M101, M102, M103

Map #57

Map #54

1221 York Avenue

Subway: 6 F Bus: M31

Map #48

1987 Adam Clayton Powell Boulevard

Map #83

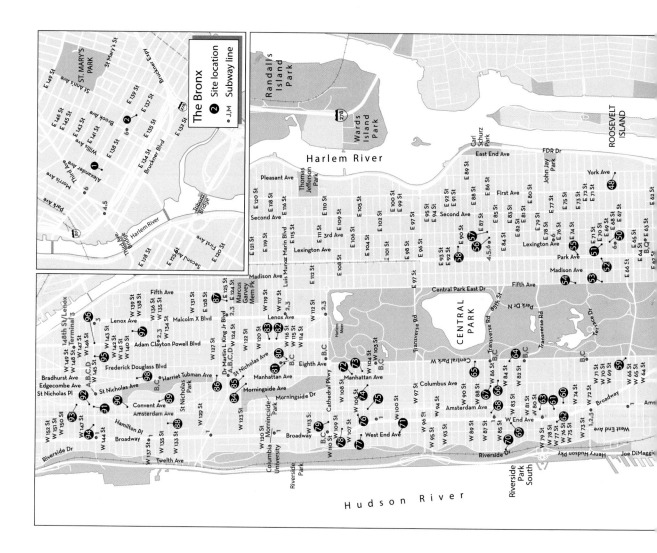

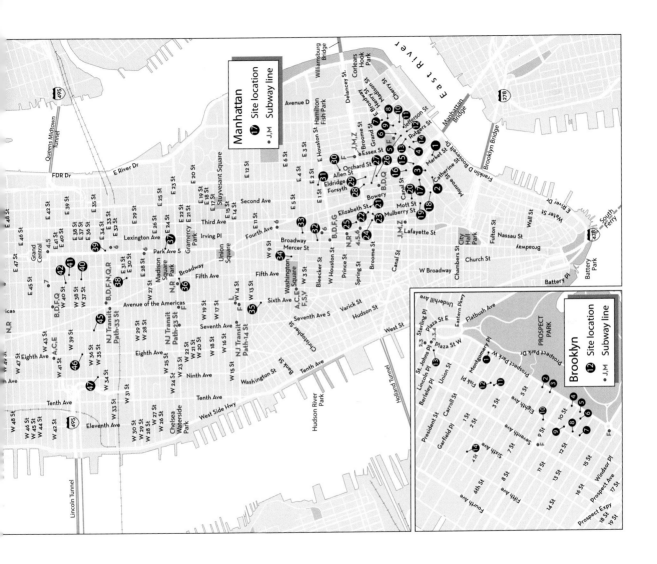

Manhattan

⑰ Site location
• J,M Subway line

Brooklyn

⑫ Site location
• J,M Subway line

ACKNOWLEDGMENTS

❧

I thank those who have suffered the walks with me in search of building detail, Elinor M. King, Jennifer Huang, and Tamera M. Gamble, as well as my two best friends, Jacqueline G. Perry and Derryck W. Brooks-Smith, who have listened to me for hours expressing my enthusiasm for architectural details throughout the city.

INDEX

❧

ANIMALS IN STONE

ARCHITECTURAL SCULPTURE IN NEW YORK CITY

W. W. NORTON
NEW YORK · LONDON

PREFACE

⚭

That which is beautiful is true; that which is true must be beautiful.   —Owen Jones

[T]he building's identity resided in the ornament.   —Louis Henri Sullivan

While completing Faces in Stone, I noticed many beautiful building details than I could not include in that book. These details were animals and creatures, and they conveyed much about the building, the architect, and, in some cases, the function within.

While many of these buildings are classified as historic landmarks and will be saved from demolition, many do not have this classification, and the details on them are just as important and have just as much artistic value as those on the historic landmark list.

When strolling down a street of buildings that were constructed during the last part of the nineteenth century, there is a visual harmony and feeling of a neighborhood that many new streets and buildings lack. Older buildings add character to the streetscape and a sense of history to the neighborhood and the individuals and groups that live there. Historic or not, they are part of America's history, and saving them is just as important as saving the historic buildings.

Nearly 24 million people immigrated to the United States between 1880 and 1920, primarily from southern and eastern Europe. (My parents were also immigrants, coming from the West Indies around 1915.) Many settled in urban areas and lived in neighborhoods that included others from their country and spoke their language. The reasons these immigrants came here vary, but they each brought skills and crafts, which are evident in many of the buildings illustrated in this book.

INTRODUCTION

by Andrew S. Dolkart

Architectural historian, author, and director, Historic Preservation Program at the Columbia University Graduate School of Architecture, Planning and Preservation

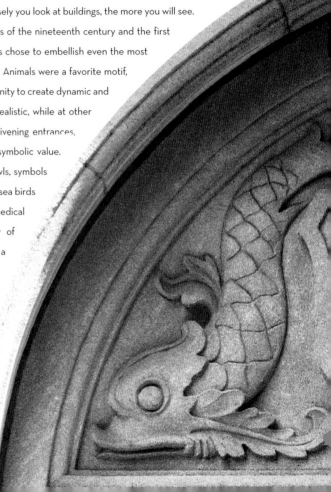

It is an unquestionable truth in New York City that the more closely you look at buildings, the more you will see. This is especially true of buildings designed in the final decades of the nineteenth century and the first decades of the twentieth century, when architects and builders chose to embellish even the most unpretentious structures with carved stone or cast terra cotta. Animals were a favorite motif, probably because they provided sculptors with a broad opportunity to create dynamic and original ornament. Sometimes these animal figures are highly realistic, while at other times they are quite fanciful. Most are simply decorative, enlivening entrances, windows, balconies, and other façade features; they have no symbolic value. Occasionally, however, the ornament reflects a specific use—owls, symbols of wisdom, on schools (105-125 Tech Place, Brooklyn); ships and sea birds on the Seamen's Bank for Savings (74 Wall Street); the medical caduceus, with a single snake, at the New York Academy of Medicine (1216 Fifth Avenue); or a caduceus with two snakes, a symbol of Mercury, god of commerce, on business buildings such as the Harriman Bank (35-39 Broadway).

Looking at the animals presented in this volume or at the thousands of others to be found on New York City buildings, the paramount question is who carved them and why? Some of the creatures illustrated here inhabit major public buildings, grand commercial structures, prestigious clubs and mansions, places designed by leading architects. A few of the carvings can actually be attributed to a specific sculptor—the Indians riding horses and hunting buffalo on the Manhattan Bridge, for example, are the work of Charles Rumsey, although just why this western scene adorns one of our urban bridges remains a mystery. But most animal sculpture is not on well-known buildings. On the contrary, almost all of the animals illustrated here reside on vernacular row houses and apartment buildings commissioned by speculative builders and generally designed by the little-known architects who specialized in this type of work. The architects chose the locations for sculpture, but they did not actually design it. Thus, we owe a great debt to the anonymous stone carvers who created the wonderful ornamental detail on our buildings. Sadly, no records survive stating who exactly was responsible for architectural carving, but most of the sculptors were probably immigrants, many from the United Kingdom in the nineteenth century, while Italians came to dominate the industry in the early twentieth century. It is these nameless men who created the rams, birds, bats, fish, and ubiquitous lion's heads that adorn so many buildings, as well as the more unusual and often whimsical pieces of architectural sculpture featured in Robert King's photographs.

Note: Unless otherwise specified, addresses are in Manhattan.

For maps showing the location of the animals and an index to the addresses, see pages 142-144.

1-9 William Street

Subway: ④ ⑤ Ⓡ Ⓝ

Bus: M1, M6, M9

Map #1

Map #5

128 Willow Street, Brooklyn

Subway: Bus: B41-LTD, B51, B61

Map #1

1103-1105 Jerome Avenue, Bronx

Subway: **4** **B** **D**   Bus: BX6, MX35

Map #3

11

107-55 Queens Boulevard, Queens

Map #4

51 West 94 Street

Subway: B C 1 2 3
Bus: M7, M96, M86

Map #80

13

39 Pierrepont Street, Brooklyn

Subway: ② ③ ④ ⑤ Ⓜ Ⓡ Bus: B41-LTD, B51, B61

Map #2

367-369 E. 149 Street, Bronx

Map #2

19-25 Eighth Avenue, Brooklyn

Map #8

52 Clark Street, Brooklyn

Subway: Bus: B51, B61

Map #3

21 East 21 Street

Subway: ④ ⑥ Ⓝ Ⓡ Ⓦ
Bus: M1, M2, M3

Map #19

19

424-432 Claremont Parkway, Bronx

Subway: Bus: BX11, BX15, BX41

Map #4

340 E. 139 Street, Bronx

Map #1

35-41 Broad Street

Subway: ④ ⑤ ⓡ ⓦ
Bus: M1, M6

Map #4

22

23

180 Eighth Avenue, Brooklyn

Subway: **2** **3** Bus: B67, B23

Map #9

680 Madison Avenue

Subway: 5 A C F M R
Bus: M1, M2-LTD

Map #54

51-55 Park Avenue

Subway:  4 5 6 7 S

Bus: M1, M103

Map #40

1874 Washington Avenue, Bronx

Subway: **B** **D**   Bus: BX15, BX36, BX55

Map #5

534-540 Flatbush Avenue, Brooklyn

Subway: Bus: B41

Map #11

Map #12

29

Map #2

29-28 41 Avenue, Queens

Subway: 7 E G V N R W Bus: Q32

Map #1

82-10 Queens Boulevard, Queens

Subway: Bus: Q58, Q59, Q60

Map #3

Map #78

33

29-33 West 36 Street

Map #31

34

Map #30

10 Sheridan Square

Subway: Bus: M2-LTD, M3, M5-LTD

Map #11

183 Lincoln Road, Brooklyn

Subway: 2 5 B Q 5

Bus: B41, B44-LTD, B49

Map #12

Map #32

Map #58

40

25-31 West 81 Street

Subug Subway: **B** **C** **1** Bus: M79, M86

Map #73

28 East 10 Street

Subway: Ⓛ Ⓝ Ⓡ Ⓠ Ⓦ
Bus: M2-LTD, M3, M5-LTD

Map #15

257 West 39 Street

Subway: ① ② ③ ⑦ Ⓝ Ⓡ Ⓠ Ⓦ Ⓢ

Bus: M4, M7, M16

Map #35

105-125 Tech Place, Brooklyn

way:  Bus: B51

Map #7

44

30 West 72 Street

Map #67

14 Gramercy Park South

Subway: Bus: M1, M3

Map #17

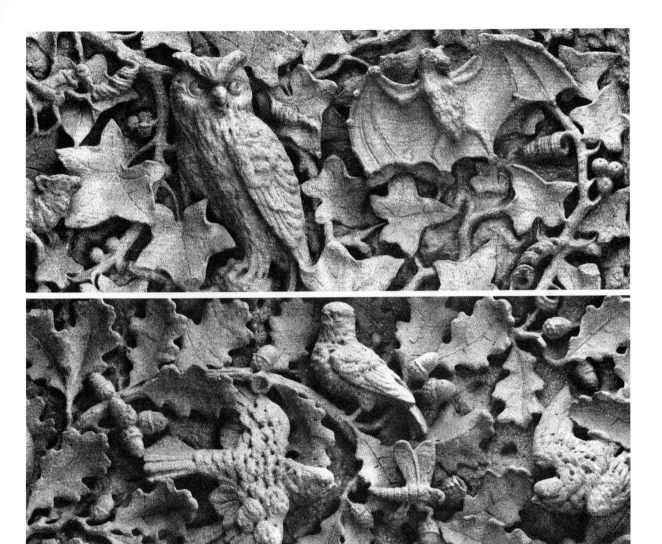

37-41 West 44 Street

Subway: 1 2 3 4 5 6 7 N R

Bus: BM1, M2-LTD, M3, M7

Map #44

40 West 72 Street

Subway: ① ② ③ Ⓑ Ⓒ

Bus: M7, M66, M72

Map #68

738 Saint Marks Avenue, Brooklyn

Subway: Ⓐ Ⓒ ③ Bus: B44-LTD, B45, B65

Map #13

51

149 East 38 Street

Subway: 4 5 6 7 S

Bus: M101, M102, M103

Map #28

157 Hudson Street

Subway: N R Q W
Bus: M6, M20, M21

Map #10

2 West 96 Street

Map #81

116-122 East 39 Street

Map #41

376-378 Lewis Avenue, Brooklyn

Subway: A C Bus: B26

Map #14

167 West 145 Street

Map #85

70 Remsen Street, Brooklyn

Map #4

730 Park Avenue

Subway: 6 F

Bus: M1,M2-LTD, M3, M101-LTD, M103

Map #59

80-90 Eighth Avenue

Subway: L 1 2 3
Bus: M7, M14A, M140

Map #13

130 East 25 Street

Map #23

63

457-459 West 150 Street

Subway: Ⓐ Ⓑ Ⓒ Ⓓ
Bus: M2-LTD, M3, M101-LTD

Map #88

Map #50

125 East 50 Street

Subway: 4 5 6 N R
Bus: M1-LTD, M2-LTD, M101, M102, M103

Map #48

127 West 96 Street

Subway: B C 1 2 3
Bus: M7, M96, M106

Map #79

163 East 70 Street

Subway: **6**

Bus: M1-LTD, M2-LTD, M101-LTD, M102, M103

Map #60

81 Eighth Avenue

Subway: L 1 2 3
Bus: M7, M14A, M14D

Map #14

239-243 Park Avenue South

Map #20

Map #34

Map #37

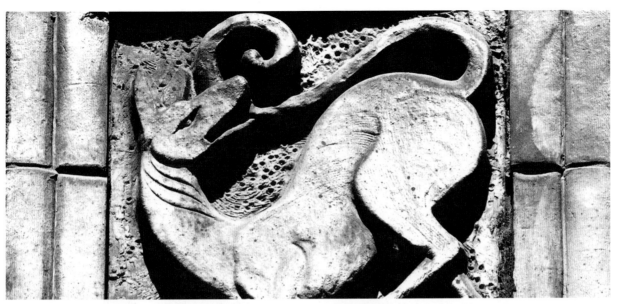

99 Nassau Street

Subway: ④ ⑤ Ⓡ Ⓦ

Bus: M6, M9, M103

Map #7

218-220 Fifth Avenue

Subway: Ⓝ Ⓡ Ⓦ ⑥
Bus: M1, M2-LTD, M3

Map #25

Map #26

242-250 Park Avenue South

Subway: ④ ⑥ Ⓝ Ⓡ Ⓠ Ⓦ Ⓛ

Bus: M1, M2, M3

Map #18

225 West 106 Street

Subway: Ⓦ Bus: M4, M5-LTD, M7

Map #83

232 Madison Avenue

Map #39

Map #70

243 Riverside Drive

Subway: ① ② ③
Bus: M5-LTD, M7, M96

Map #77

661 West End Avenue

Subway: 1 2 3

Bus: M5-LTD, M7, M86

Map #76

Map #26

Subway: **2** **5** Bus: BXM4B, BX34

Map #6

Map #42

251-257 West 87 Street

Subway: ① ② ③ Ⓑ Ⓒ

Bus: M7, M86, M104

Map #74

Map #8

115 East 67 Street

Subway: ④ ⑤ ⑥ Ⓝ Ⓡ
Bus: M1- oLTD, M2-LTD, M101, M102, M103

Map #57

91

Map #69

36 East 22 Street

Subway: ④ ⑥ Ⓝ Ⓡ Ⓦ
Bus: M1, M2-LTD, M3

Map #21

302 Fifth Avenue

Map #27

Map #56

463 Seventh Avenue

Subway: Ⓑ Ⓓ Ⓕ Ⓥ Ⓝ Ⓡ Ⓠ Ⓦ

Bus: M2, M3, M7

Map #33

340 West 72 Street

Subway: 1 2 3
Bus: M5-LTD, M7, M72

Map #71

Map #75

358 West End Avenue

Subway: ① ② ③
Bus: M7, M5-LTD, M79, M104

Map #72

366-370 Madison Avenue

Subway: 4 5 6 7 S
Bus: M1, M2-LTD, M3

Map #45

101

Map #82

386 Park Avenue South

Subway: ⑥ Ⓝ Ⓡ Ⓦ
Bus: M1, M2-LTD, M103

Map #24

571-575 Park Avenue

Subway: 4 5 6 N R

Bus: M1, M2-LTD, M101-LTD, M103

Map #55

Map #16

475 Fifth Avenue

Map #43

557-565 Lexington Avenue

Subway: **4** **5** **6** **7** **S**
Bus: M101-LTD, M102, M103

Map #49

523-527 Lexington Avenue

Subway:

Bus: M101-LTD, M102, M103

Map #46

391-393 Fifth Avenue

Subway: B D F V N R Q W
Bus: M1, M2-LTD, M3

Map #38

539-555 Lexington Avenue

Subway: ④ ⑤ ⑥ ⑦ Ⓢ
Bus: M101-LTD, M102, M103

Map #47

525 Seventh Avenue

Map #36

114

516 West 142 Street

Map #86

Map #51

911-917 Seventh Avenue

Map #53

Map #22

927 Fifth Avenue

Subway: 6

Bus: M1, M2-LTD, M3, M101-LTD

Map #62

121

1710 Broadway

Subway:  N R Q W

Bus: M3, M7, M50

Map #52

1165 Fifth Avenue

Map #65

124

Map #10

1216 Fifth Avenue

Subway: **6**
Bus: M1, M2-LTD, M3

YGIEA

ASCLEF

Map #66

1040 Park Avenue

Subway: ④ ⑤ ⑥
Bus: M2-LTD, M3, M86, M101-LTD

Map #63

Map #89

2184 Eighth Avenue

Subway: ② ③ Ⓑ Ⓒ
Bus: M2-LTD, M3, M7, M101-LTD

Map #84

2802-2824 Frederick Douglass Blvd.

Map #87

Manhattan Bridge

Subway: 6 N R Q W

Bus: M6, M9, M103

Map #9

133 East 87 Street

Subway: ④ ⑤ ⑥
Bus: M1, M2-LTD, M101-LTD, M103

Map #64

Map #61

161-167 Sands Street, Brooklyn

Subway: Ⓐ Ⓒ Ⓕ Bus: B51, B61, B75

Map #6

142 Joralemon Street, Brooklyn

Map #5

65 Beaver Street

Subway: 4 5 R W
Bus: M6, M9

Map #2

Map #6

74 Wall Street

Subway: ④ ⑤ Ⓡ Ⓦ
Bus: M6, M9

Map #3

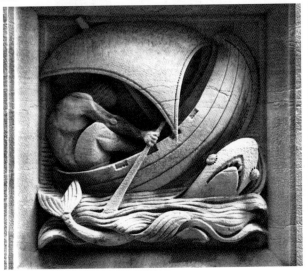

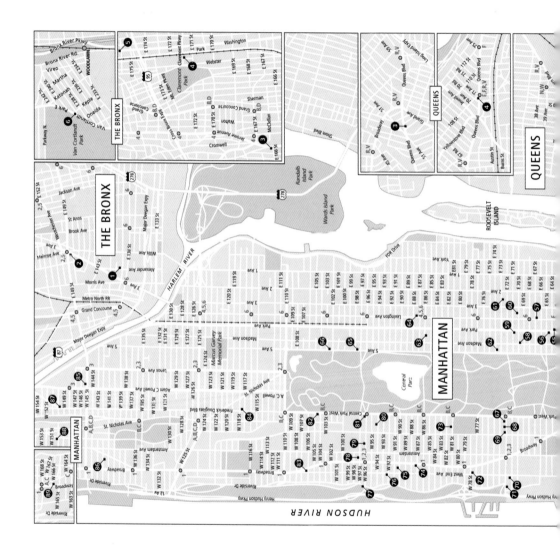

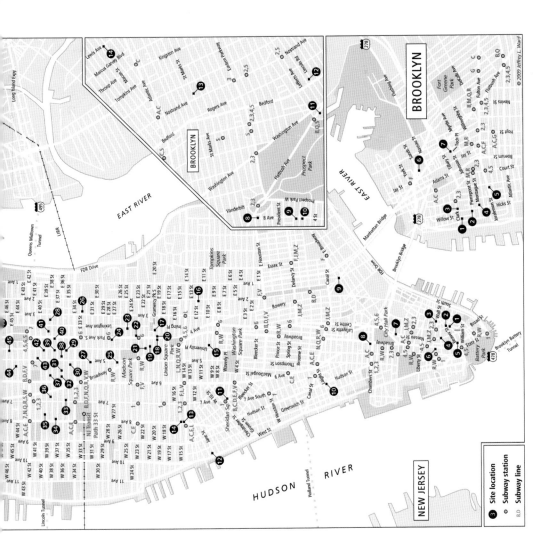

ACKNOWLEDGMENTS

❧❧❧

My thanks go to two people—Mel Rosenthal and Amy Robinson, both instructors at the Empire State College in New York City—for helping me sharpen my photographic achievements, skills, and critical faculties.

INDEX

❧❧❧